# FORRES and AREA
## PAST & PRESENT

Compiled by
Mike Seton

Photography by
Peter Bonar

SUB·SPE

Moray District Libraries
1982

# ACKNOWLEDGEMENTS

We are deeply indebted to all those people, too many to list individually, in Forres and the surrounding area who made photographs available for publication. Without them this book would not have been possible. Special thanks are due to Alexander Gollan, chairman of the Forres Community Council and to Lambert Munro, chairman of the Findhorn and Kinloss Community Council for their work in collecting material and providing information. Forres is more fortunate than most towns of its size in having had its own newspaper since 1837: the files of the "Forres Gazette" are a great storehouse of fact and contemporary comment which have proved invaluable in the compilation of this book.

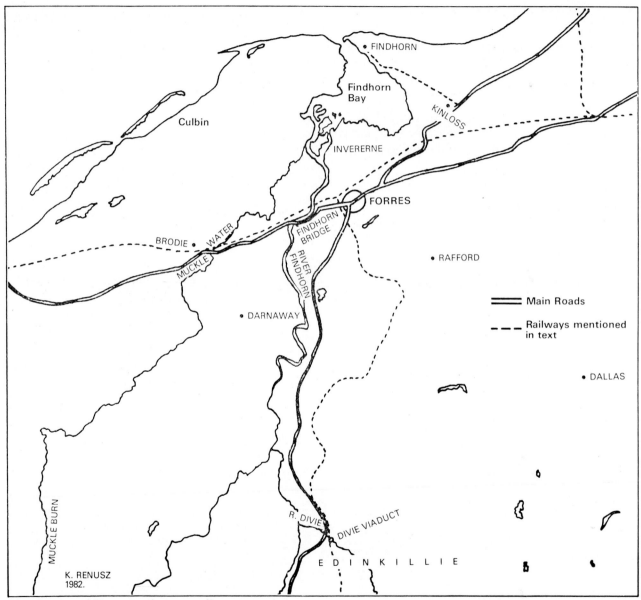

Sketch map of Forres and surrounding area.

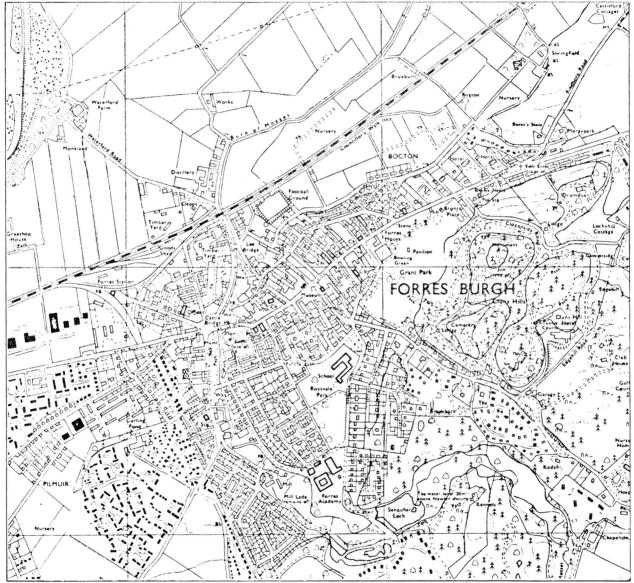

Plan of the town of Forres.

Sueno's Stone is the tallest remaining sculptured
stone made in Scotland during the early medieval
period. It was possibly erected during the ninth
century to commemorate an heroic battle campaign
as yet unknown. The Cassieford Dovecote probably
belonged to the Bogton estate and was of the oblong
type with the door facing south. In its latter days it
was owned by the Earl of Moray but rabbits
apparently undermined the walls and consequently it
was razed to the ground.

1

The original proposal in 1806 for a memorial to Nelson was to erect a tower that would "form a most agreeable object to every traveller and the country at large, a useful sea beacon, an excellent observatory, and a commanding alarm post in the event of an enemy's approach by sea or land." The four large cannon in the old photographs were made at Carron in 1806, gifted to Forres in 1901, and melted down to make munitions in the last war. The two small cannon are said to have been at the bombardment of Alexandria in 1882.

The large building in the right background of the old photograph is the chemical works, destroyed by fire in 1896. Made of wood, the works formed an immense parallelogram covering about an acre of ground, but were reduced to a total wreck in little more than two hours. At the time of the fire, sulphuric acid ran into the Mosset Burn killing all the trout.

The new photograph has the present St Laurence and St Leonard's churches. St Leonard's, formerly the United Free High Church, was built in 1902 to a design by Ross and McBeth of Inverness at a cost of £8,400. The foundation stone was laid by a famous son of Forres, Lord Strathcona (see no. 29), who was presented on the occasion with a silver trowel.

The Lodge St John (Operative) no. 37 was founded in 1706 and at one time owned several properties in the town, the last of these being an old building near the Red Lion Hotel. The present Temple was built in 1926 with funds raised by its members, most notably £1000 from a bazaar held in September 1924. The older photograph shows the laying of the foundation stone by the Earl of Elgin and Kincardine, a one-time Grand Master of Scotland, on February 10th, 1926. The Temple, which has a frontage of dressed Newton stone, was estimated to have cost £2500 and was designed by Peter Fulton's son, Robert (see 10 and 20).

4

Episcopalian services in Forres were for many years held in private houses conducted by visiting clergymen until 1841 when the church of St John the Evangelist was opened. This building, now the oldest place of worship in current use in the town, was designed by Patrick Wilson of Inverness in the Italianate style with a campanile or square tower. It is built in the shape of a Latin Cross and is internally high and narrow. A new chapel in the north transept was consecrated in September 1969. At the same time the gallery, which had been closed because it was unsafe, was repaired and re-opened thanks to a donation from Brodie of Brodie.

Forres House, or "The Great Lodging" as it was sometimes called, was originally the town house of the Tullochs of Tannachy. Having passed through a succession of owners and several reconstructions, after the First World War it came into the possession of the Town Council largely through the generosity of Sir Alexander Grant, a native of the town, who was also the donor of the National Library in Edinburgh. The grounds, 32 acres in extent, were laid out as a public park, named Grant Park, and formally opened on 27th August 1924, on which day Sir Alexander was given the freedom of the burgh. The House, part of which was rented for a short time by Maurice Walsh, the author, served the town for many years as a community centre housing the baths, registrar and many clubs and societies until in 1970 it was destroyed by fire. A sunken garden designed by Alistair Sinclair was constructed on the site in 1971 whilst a new community centre, also called Forres House, was built in 1973 just a few yards from the old.

The "Academical Institution" was started in 1829 in the Anderson's Institution building on the corner of High Street and South Street. In 1877 an additional school was built on the north side of the High Street roughly where the Community Centre is now. It was demolished in 1970. In 1926 the Academy was provided with a new building which retained the old Anderson's Institution frontage. The properties in front of the school on the very left of the older photograph were demolished in 1964. Some five years later the Academy moved to its present site at Burdsyards Road and in 1971 the Anderson's Institution buildings were renovated and altered and became Anderson's Primary School.

The Queen's Hotel is probably the oldest hotel in
continuous use as such in Forres, although the
present name is of relatively recent vintage. Dr
Johnson is said to have stayed here overnight,
though there is no evidence for this. The "Defiance"
and "Star" mail coaches stopped here en route
between Aberdeen and Inverness. The main building
of the Royal Bank on the opposite side of the street
dates from 1681. It was reconstructed in 1843 to
house a branch of the National Bank and in 1973
further altered to accommodate the Royal Bank.

Caroline Street is said to have been named after Queen Caroline and was at one time known as Shambles Wynd. Here was situated in the 1870s a clay pipe factory whose "Swinyard" brand of pipes was widely used throughout the North of Scotland. The property on the corner of Caroline Street and High Street opposite the Carlton Hotel had in its front window for many years a large clock from which many Forresians took the time of day. Made by George Cunningham, a well-known Forres jeweller who died in 1911, the clock was moved in 1952 to Morayshire Motors (now Dicksons) and in 1979 installed in the golf club-house at Muiryshade.

In 1838 A. C. Audsley opened the Plough Inn on this site. In 1900 the building, then known as the Moray Arms, was demolished and redeveloped as an hotel and two shops to the design of Peter Fulton, who was also the architect of the Castle Bridge. The brothers Forsyth, owners of the hotel in 1923, installed a wireless for their guests, only the second such apparatus in the town. About 1930 the then owner, William Grigor, a native of Dallas who had a large wine and spirit business in Inverness, renamed it the Carlton Hotel. Greenlees opened their shoe shop, still in the hands of their successors, in 1908.

10

Alexander Falconer of Calcutta, whose residence was in Tolbooth Street, died in 1856 leaving £1,000 to establish a museum in Forres. His brother, Hugh, a scientist of some distinction, bequeathed a further £500 and a large collection of bones and fossils, mostly from India. By 1863 the site for the Museum had been identified in Tolbooth Street, but it was not until 1869 that it was actually built, to a design of Alexander Reid of Elgin with decorative sculpture by Thomas Goodwillie. The museum was run for many years by a board of trustees until it came under the control of the District Council in 1975, since when it has attracted record attendances.

An interesting sidelight is presented by a complaint to the Police Commissioners in 1891 that the passage of large numbers of cows down Tolbooth Street made such a mess as to make life impossible for pedestrians.

In March 1935 William Joyce, later notorious as "Lord Haw-Haw" addressed a small meeting of British Fascists in the Museum Square.

The foundation stone of the present Tolbooth was laid in 1838. The architect for the new building was William Robertson, whose design was based on that of the previous early eighteenth century building on the same site. The adjoining former prison was completed about 1849.

In front of the Tolbooth is the Market Cross. Resembling the Scott Monument in Edinburgh, it was designed by Thomas MacKenzie of Elgin and erected in 1844. It is on the same site as the previous cross and incorporates the basement-stone of its predecessor in its construction.

One of the most distinctive features of the north side of this part of the High Street is the rock-dressed freestone frontage of the premises of MacKenzie & Cruickshank, who although they owned the property for over half a century previously and used part of it as a store only moved into the whole building in 1963. Prior to this their business had been conducted from the former branch of the City of Glasgow Bank at number 74 High Street. Number 107 High Street was at one time the offices of the British Linen Bank before they moved across the road to the building now owned by the Clydesdale Bank. Cumming Street dates from about 1820 and was named after John Cumming, banker, who bought the existing close and redeveloped it to form a street.

13

HIGH STREET, FORRES, LOOKING W. 11,754. G.W.W.

The area near the Market Cross on the south side of the High Street has been a centre of financial activity in the town for many years. The present Bank of Scotland was opened in 1854 as a branch of the Caledonian Bank. It was designed by Thomas Mackenzie, the architect of the Market Cross. The North of Scotland Bank opened a branch next door at number 100 in 1898 in premises previously occupied by James Gray, tailor and clothier. It is now the offices of Geoffrey Smith and Partners, surveyors and valuers. The building adjoining this was erected in 1839 as premises for the British Linen Bank who had established the first branch bank north of the Tay in Forres in the mid-eighteenth century. The building is now a branch of the Clydesdale Bank.

The church seen in the old photograph dated from 1775, a building with "no pretension of elegant architecture" to which Forres Town Council contributed half the cost. By 1896 it was apparent that this building had had its day and the congregation resolved to build a new one. The foundation stone for the present building, designed by John Robertson of Inverness, was laid by Lord Strathcona on 17th August, 1904, the Moderator of the General Assembly conducting the Dedication service of the completed buiding on 1st March, 1906. Two old bells, dating from 1682 and 1781 respectively, were transferred from the old building to the new which also contains a chime of eight bells cast in 1905 by John C. Wilson of Glasgow.

This close at 152 High Street was once the site of the "Cleekim Inn". The shop at the head of the close has the distinction of being the oldest inhabited shop and house in Forres and dates from 1668. In 1851 the property was occupied by Duncan Riach, tailor, who took over from Stuart & Simpson, cabinetmakers and later moved eastward to Warden's Buildings. In 1862 Alexander Taylor opened his bakery here, with the bakehouse at the foot of the close, selling a "fine four pound loaf" for seven pence. The shop is currently run by Mr James Grant who took over as sole partner on the retirement of Miss Florence Longmuir in 1981.

16

"The Green Roadie", as it was familiarly called, was a private road, the property of the Castlehill Church. At one time the site of a close of houses, the road, although gated at both ends, was usually open to the public. However, in March 1923, following vandalism to the Church railings, the road was closed "until further notice", only being opened on Sundays for the convenience of the congregation. In 1934 the congregation sold the road to the town council who had it widened, involving the demolition of the sweet shop at 172 High Street, surfaced, lined with trees and named Castlehill Road.

High Street, West End, Forres

The post office buildings erected in 1911 were the ninth to be used for that purpose in Forres. There was disappointment at the time that "one of the wealthiest departments of state should have been permitted to erect in so prominent a position such a striking monument of their cheeseparing policy." The Forres Gazette was however, impressed by the telegraphic installation which enabled them to publish detailed reports of the Chancellor's Budget statement within two hours of him finishing his speech.

Castlehill Church, which had celebrated its centenary in November 1971, had to close a few months later. It reopened in 1980. During the intervening period it had been used by the Free Church congregation.

Castlehill is the site of the ancient castle of Forres, an important stronghold for Scotland's early kings. By the late seventeenth century the castle had become ruinous, many of the stones being used to build houses in the town. In the eighteenth century William Dawson, a merchant and Provost of Forres, began the building of a mansion on the site, but financial problems caused him to abandon its construction with the walls a little over nine feet high. The partly finished house stood until 1934 when, thanks to the generosity of Sir Alexander Grant who had acquired the property, the area was made into a public park by the town council.

Castle Bridge is first mentioned in 1607, though at
this time it was only a footbridge. It was rebuilt
after the Moray floods of 1829 with a roadway 23
feet wide and two arches each of 24 feet 3 inches
span. In 1907 the town council decided to build a
new bridge. Peter Fulton, who was also responsible
for the Carlton Hotel (no. 10), was appointed
architect. The new bridge was to have a roadway
42ft wide and was constructed with stone from
Cummingston and Newton. The bridge was opened
with great ceremony on 16th July, 1908.

Victoria Hotel, Forres, Morayshire.

In 1864 Joseph Logan, a local businessman with a confectioner's shop near the Tolbooth, built the Station Hotel in a prime position close to the railway station and at the junction of six roads. It was erected on the site of the old horse-market stance to a design by George Petrie of Elgin which included plans for a fountain on the then triangular shaped plot at the front of the building. In 1886 it was taken over by Alexander Cameron, formerly head boots at the Gordon Arms Hotel in Elgin and renamed "Victoria". In more recent years the hotel has been owned by the large national firms of Thomas Usher & Sons and, currently, Lorimers Breweries of Edinburgh.

At the same time as the inauguration of the Agricultural Hall opposite was the opening on the first day of the Forres Show, 1867 of Taylor's Railway and County Hotel. Appropriately the first function to be held in the new hotel was a dinner to the Fat Cattle Club. Renamed the Royal Hotel in 1873 it was taken over in 1889 by Alexander Macdonald, a town councillor who was also lessee of the station refreshment rooms at Aberdeen where Queen Victoria dined on her journeys to and from Balmoral. The hotel was famous for its gardens and for a rather talkative parrot much given to calling for a "glass of whisky for Polly". A dining-room and eight bedrooms were added in 1896 and the hotel is presently one of the largest in the town.

FORRES, FROM THE CHEMICAL WORKS. 11,787 B.W.W.

The older photograph was taken from the chemical works (see no. 3) which provided a vantage point not available to the modern photographer. The skyline is still dominated by the Nelson Tower and the Tolbooth with the notable addition since the early photograph of St Laurence's Church. Prominent in the foreground of the older photograph are the railway and original station buildings. The first railway line into Forres was the Inverness and Aberdeen Junction Railway which reached Forres from Inverness in 1858. In 1863 the Inverness and Perth Junction Railway was opened connecting Forres with Perth. This necessitated the building of a new station at Forres, the original station buildings being used as the stationmaster's residence.

Taylor's Mills were started in the early 1840s by the Taylor family, the most prominent member of which was Peter Taylor, provost of Forres from 1872 to 1875 and a leader of the strong local temperance movement. The factory produced various sorts of woollen goods including tweeds known throughout the country and even exported to Australia, "the threads so spun and woven that the fabric wears twice as long as anything of the same kind produced elsewhere". The mills were also well known for a particular kind of rug made from the "salvages of cloth" and known as a "Brodie". In 1971 the chimney and buildings on the left of the older photograph were bought by the Town Council and demolished. The buildings on the right were converted and opened as the Mosset Tavern in 1975.

The Mosset burn has been a source of prosperity and on occasion difficulty for Forres throughout the course of history. It has provided power, water and drainage for a brewery, a chemical works and for a woollen, corn, flour and saw mills. It has also needed the expense of straightening, cleaning and bridging and from time to time has flooded parts of the town.

On the west bank of the burn, between the Lee and Castle Bridge, where the nurseries are, is the site of the Cholera hospital. Built in the 1830s soon after the disease first appeared in Britain it was temporarily used as a jail in 1840 and later became the Burnside Home for old people. In 1950 Auchernack House in the High Street was acquired as an old people's home and Burnside was demolished.

The Kirk Wynd, leading from the Parish Church to the Burn Green was probably the main route from Forres via the Lee Bridge to Waterford and the crossing place of Findhorn. There is a tradition that this street was formed by Cromwell's soldiers leading their horses to drink at the burn. In the nineteenth century it was named Gordon Street after Charles Gordon, wine merchant and Provost from 1830-35, who had his premises there.

The Burn Green was used as a drying green for blankets from the woollen mills and for washing from the Hand Laundry, the rear elevation of which is prominent in the centre of the older photograph.

26

Familiarly known as "The Big Hoose", number 100 North Road, or North Back Street, was demolished in 1950. It is said that it was once an inn where stage coaches stopped on their way to cross the Findhorn at Waterford. From about 1860 until a few years before its demolition it was a hand laundry, where, when business was heavy, the employees would work until 10.30 p.m. and then start again at 2.30 the next morning. Throughout the years the walls were tapped by numerous fortune hunters, but demolition scotched the legend that a fortune was built into the masonry.

27

This quaint, semi-circular building was known as the Keith Bread Shop and came into being in the late 1850s when large numbers of navvies were employed locally in railway construction. The local bakers being unable to cope with the demand, bread was sent from Keith every night by horse-drawn cart and sold from this shop. The upper storey of the building was reached by a narrow, winding stone stair not easily negotiated by large people. Despite its unusual architecture, the building was demolished in 1952. The large new building on the right in the new photograph is the sheltered housing for the elderly built in 1975.

More than one place in Moray claims to be the birthplace of Donald A. Smith, later Lord Strathcona. In September 1900 he admitted in a speech at Forres to "having been born and passing my schooldays in this town". The house in which he was born is given as that shown here which was demolished to make way for the new Castle Bridge in 1908 (see no. 20). Donald Smith made his name and fortune in Canada with the Hudson Bay Company, and eventually became Canadian High Commissioner in London. On the opposite bank of the Mosset is the war memorial, made of stone from Wester New Forres, surmounted by a bronze figure, it was unveiled on 23rd August, 1922. The figure was designed by the Edinburgh sculptor Alexander Carrick, and is 7 feet 8 inches in height.

The older photograph shows
how, prior to the building of the
Castlehill housing scheme, a
clear view could be had of the
Thomson monument on the
Castlehill. James Thomson was
a military surgeon and Crimean
War hero whose connections
were actually across the Firth in
Cromarty. However his friend,
Sir James MacGrigor, Director-
General of the Army Medical
Department, being frustrated in
his ambition to erect a memorial
in Cromarty, decided instead on
the Castlehill, of which he was
at that time the proprietor.
The Castlehill housing scheme,
which included the first blocks
of flats Forres town council had
ever built, received a Saltire
Award in 1959.

In July 1964 The Picture House, the only cinema in Forres, closed down and the building turned into a furniture store and depot. The cinema had come to Forres in 1913 when the Lyceum opened in Caroline Street later to be replaced by the Picture House. The first "talkie" was shown in September 1930. The YMCA building was closed in 1963. It was bought by the Town Council and demolished to make way for Hainings Road and the Council housing seen on the left in the new photograph. The Forres Cycling Club rooms on the right were opened in 1972 partly financed by a grant from the Council. Houses at the foot of the street where the car park is now were demolished in 1964.

The fame of hydropathy originated with the work of Vincent Priessnitz, a farmer of Grafenberg in Silesia. The Clunyhill Hydropathic was built on Dean's Hill and formally opened on 14th August 1865. It offered Turkish baths as well as ordinary in an area with a dry, genial climate in which "the amount of ozone is high on average, an element of peculiar value in the restoration and preservation of health".

A new east wing was added about 1892 and a new west wing in 1899. The building was taken over by the military in World War II and later became the property of North British Hotels who extensively modernised the premises. Later it was sold to Allied Hotels and in 1975 to the Findhorn Foundation to use as an education centre.

Drumduan House was built by Simon Fraser and in 1845 was advertised as "of chaste architectural design, built a few years ago of the best materials, regardless of expense, to ensure comfort." In 1825 workmen digging a new road on the Drumduan estate about 200 yards east of the Nelson Monument found the skeleton of a soldier shot there for desertion some 80 years before. The story goes that he was led out from the jail on a St. Lawrence Market day dressed in his grave clothes and less than an hour after he had been executed a runner, who had dallied at an inn on the way, arrived with a reprieve for him. Drumduan was acquired in 1978 by the Findhorn Foundation who have since renovated the property.

33

A meeting of those interested in the erection of what was then called a "cottage hospital" was held in the Court House on 26th September 1888. "A Friend of Forres", namely Sir Donald A. Smith, offered £5,000 and acquired a suitable site from the Town Council. The hospital, named Leanchoil after the farm under the shadow of Cairngorm where Sir Donald's mother was born, was opened in 1892. The first case admitted was a young farm servant, who was removed from a bothy on a neighbouring farm suffering from an acute attack of inflammation. In 1926 central heating, electric lights and x-ray equipment were introduced. There were further major changes in 1963, including the addition of an out-patient department, partially financed by the bequest of Mr Edward of Sanquhar.

The first Free Church in Rafford was built soon after the Disruption in 1843. Though a sound enough structure it soon became a victim of dry rot and by 1887 it was found necessary to build a replacement. The new church, opened in 1889, was erected immediately behind its predecessor and for a short time until the earlier building was demolished, both churches stood within a few yards of each other as the older photograph shows. Following the union of the United Free Church and the Church of Scotland this building became superfluous and, after many years of fund-raising, was purchased by the local community and opened as a district hall in 1950.

Until the beginning of the last century the hamlet of Dolais Mychel was situated at Torechastle on the right bank of the Lossie. The sixteen families there at the time were removed and in 1811 the present village was feued and the building began. In the notorious Moray floods of 1829 the water from the swollen River Lossie swept down the main street at a height of three feet and some 120 people had to be evacuated. By 1871 the village boasted 50 houses most of which were rebuilt in the first quarter of this century.

The Forres to Aviemore section of the main railway line from Inverness to Perth was opened in August 1863 with a significant reduction in cost and time over the previous route via Aberdeen. The most difficult engineering work was the crossing of the Divie achieved by means of this "airy handsome-looking" viaduct which cost about £9000. The piers were built of gneiss from the bed of the river and the coping of the arches and the parapets of Nairn freestone. The entire length of the structure is nearly 500 feet and trains ran about 120 feet above the bed of the river. In 1898 a more direct route from Inverness to Aviemore was opened via Carrbridge enabling the line over the Divie to be closed to passenger traffic on October 18th, 1965 despite local protests.

The present Darnaway Castle, home of the Earl of Moray, although on an ancient site, is no older than the early years of the nineteenth century. The earlier castle was probably begun for Archibald Douglas, Earl of Moray, who was killed in 1455, and finished for James II. The only surviving part of this building is the great banqueting hall, known as Randolph's Hall, built about 1450 and reportedly capable of holding 1000 armed men. By the end of the eighteenth century the castle was in such a ruinous state that the decision was taken to demolish it and build afresh. The new building, designed by Alexander Laing for Francis, the 9th Earl, cost £12,000 and was completed in 1812. It is not open to the public.

Brodie Castle has been continuously occupied by the same family for more than 400 years. It was built in 1576 and has been much added to since, though there have been Brodies at Brodie since 1160. The original entrance to the castle was by way of a first-storey door in the High Hall reached by ladder. In 1645 supporters of Montrose burned the Castle and many of the family archives were destroyed.

William, the 22nd Brodie of Brodie, carried out many alterations and additions to the property in the first half of last century. In 1980 the Castle was handed over to the National Trust. Since then tens of thousands of visitors have been able to enjoy viewing the building and the many treasures it contains.

From the wealth of archaeological discoveries which have been made in the district, it is clear that Culbin was inhabited from very early days. The ancient barony of Culbin covered thousands of acres of some of the finest land in Moray but was gradually overcome by sand until "a scene of greater desolation and dreariness would be impossible to conceive." About 1839 Grant of Kincorth tried the experiment of planting trees on the sands and other properties followed suit. However, little real progress was made until the Forestry Commission bought part of the area in 1921. Now there are mature woodlands covering an area some seven miles long and two miles wide.

The laying of the foundation stone on 1st March 1832 of the suspension bridge across the Findhorn was an event of great importance locally since it removed the uncertainty and inconvenience of relying on crossing the river by ford. Thus a crowd of about five thousand witnessed the ceremony and the cannon on Cluny Hill fired a salute. Locally called "the Chine Brig" because of the heavy chains which supported the roadway, the bridge cost a total of £10,000. Two small cottages, the Boathill Cottages, were built by the bridge. One of these was the toll house, tolls being charged until the debt on the bridge was paid off in 1881. The present bridge was opened without ceremony in 1938 after which the old bridge, despite protests from Forres Town Council, was taken down.

Invererne House, formerly known as Tannachy, was erected by General Grant in 1818 and was for several years the residence of Charles St. John, the celebrated sportsman and naturalist. The land was owned by the Tulloch family, whose town house was Forres House, for about 250 years until 1772 when it was sold to Alexander Urquhart of Maryland, USA. His brother sold it in 1817 to General Grant.

During the Moray floods of 1829 Invererne House was one of the few places left above the waters. In 1833 the house was described as "modern and particularly commodious, being in every way suited to a large Establishment". Colonel Grant Peterkin, who took over the estate in 1834 changed its name from Tannachy to Invererne. The house is currently the home of Mrs Grant Peterkin. It is not open to the public.

Kinloss has changed dramatically over the last few decades although the Kirkton has changed much less than surrounding parts. In the older photographs the huts of the smithy can be seen in front of the church. Perhaps it was these that the editor of the local newspaper was referring to when he wrote in 1866 that "the fair proportions of the church would come out much more if some ugly nuisances which come very close on it were removed." The cottages on the right, now the Abbey Inn, were occupied by farm servants and railway employees. They were thatched until 1952. Kinloss is now a well-known name nationally as a result of the activities of the large R.A.F. station there.

After the Reformation the buildings of Kinloss Abbey gradually fell into a state of disrepair and in 1574 the steeple of the Abbey Church collapsed. The buildings suffered further with the removal of many stones to build Cromwell's fort at Inverness and by the attentions of local people who used the Abbey as a convenient quarry. By 1844 the ruins were "a disgrace to a civilised community" and an attempt was made to have them placed under government protection, but this failed when the government felt unable to spend public money on their preservation. Since then there has been further decay and in 1981 a large section of the wall of the former Abbot's house collapsed.

The older photograph shows the line of the short-lived Findhorn Railway. Started in 1859, it joined the main line at Kinloss by 1860 with an initial timetable of five trains a day each way, though this was fairly soon reduced to three. It was never a profitable venture and closed in 1869, the rails being lifted in 1873 to pay off one of its many debts. The old station house, identified by its arched entrance, is still to be seen between Kilravock House and the Kimberley Inn.

In the mid-ground, in front of the church, can be seen the toll cottage, situated just before the road divides. The church was built in 1843 as the Free Church for the parish of Kinloss.

The present village is the third to bear the name Findhorn and was at one time a port of some importance, building its own ships and trading with many countries. Prior to the advent of the railways, goods were most efficiently moved over long distances by sea. In 1848 the schooner "Swift" was able to carry a cargo of cattle from Findhorn to London in only three days. By the 1880s though Findhorn presented a picture of decay and in 1923 when a steamer landed a cargo of livestock for Logie, it was noted as being "a sight unknown to the younger generation."

As early as 1857 Findhorn is described as the "fashionable sea-side rendezvous for the district" with the writer going on to propose the construction of salt-water baths for invalids. Late in the same century, though, another writer describes the village as "solemn, silent" and "wholly given over to meditation." The appearance of the village has changed in detail over the years. Electricity was introduced in 1949; there was road widening in 1966; and the last thatched roof disappeared during the 1970s. On the left in the old photograph is Mrs. Robertson's shop, since demolished, and on the right the house which at one time served as the village post-office.

47

# SELECT BIBLIOGRAPHY

| | |
|---|---|
| *Algie, M. J.* | A guide to Forres. 1887 |
| *Bain, G.* | The Culbin Sands. n.d. |
| *Bain, G.* | The River Findhorn. 1911 |
| *Cochrane, R. ed.* | Findhorn: a Scottish village. 1981 |
| *Douglas, R.* | Annals of the Royal Burgh of Forres. 1934 |
| *Forbes, A.* | Forres: A Royal Burgh 1150-1975. 1975 |
| *Howat, A. J. and Seton, M.* | Churches of Moray. 1981 |
| *Seton, M.* | Moray past and present. 1978 |
| *Shaw, L.* | History of the Province of Moray. New ed., 1882 |
| *Hamilton, H. ed.* | Third Statistical Account of Scotland Counties of Moray and Nairn. 1965 |
| *Tranter, N.* | The North-East. 1974 |
| *Watson, J. & W.* | Morayshire described. 1868 |
| *Elgin Courant* | 1836-1967 |
| *Forres Gazette* | 1837-date |
| *Northern Scot* | 1880-date |